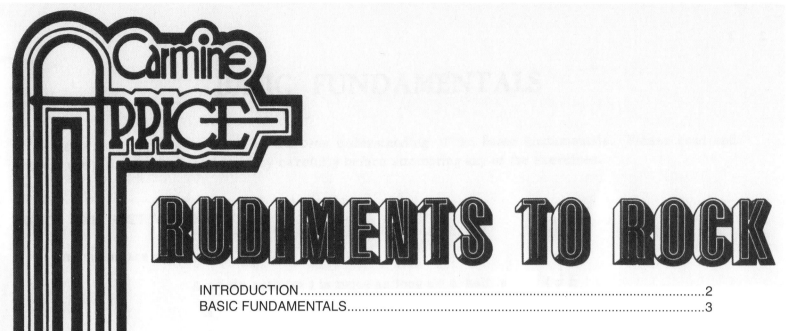

Carmine Appice
RUDIMENTS TO ROCK

**Subscribe to *Modern Drummer*, the world's best drumming magazine, at:
www.moderndrummer.com/subscribe**

**For fun and educational videos, subscribe to the
"Modern Drummer Official" YouTube channel.**

Modern Drummer Publisher/CEO **David Frangioni**

Managing Director/SVP **David Hakim**

Published by:
Modern Drummer Publications, Inc.
315 Ridgedale Ave #478
East Hanover, NJ 07936

INTRODUCTION

This basic drum book was designed specifically to provide beginning drum students with fresh ideas and procedures. The objective of this approach, through these exercises and explanations, is to develop the novice percussionist from the most basic fundamentals and then progress to the more difficult, modern beats so characteristic of much of today's music. The basics in reading, hand control, various triplet feelings and modern rock beats are all contained in this publication. This book is based on many years of experience in teaching percussionists, thereby learning the needs of students in order to develop and coordinate hands, feet and mind. This type of book provides the raw material and thereby will hopefully prove to be very beneficial to the beginning and developing drum student.

From the Publisher

Carmine Appice is a true drumming legend. Carmine was not only one of rock's first drum heroes, he was also an inspiration to me as a child. The moment I picked up Realistic Rock, I was hooked! (I subsequently collected all of his books, but Realistic Rock was my first Carmine drum book.)

I remember that it had a picture of Carmine's double-bass maple drumkit with a gong drum over the floor toms, double China cymbals upside down, electronic drums above the rack toms…I could go on and on. I was inspired, and I hadn't even opened the book yet! Once inside this treasure trove of rock rhythms and concepts, I found a virtually endless vocabulary available from which to draw new ideas and to perfect the important, solid playing that every drummer needs to know.

The benefit of working through Carmine's catalog is that it improves your playing quickly. You will save enormous amounts of time by practicing his exercises. This is the formula to fast-track your rock drumming prowess!

Modern Drummer is proud to present the entire Carmine Appice catalog, which to this day still inspires our playing! Enjoy, and we wish you the best always on your drumming journey.

David Frangioni
CEO/Publisher of Modern Drummer Publications, Inc.

BASIC FUNDAMENTALS

It is most important that we have a keen understanding of the basic fundamentals. Please read and digest the following explanations very carefully before attempting any of the exercises.

NOTE AND REST VALUES:*

All notes are assigned certain time values:

A whole note (o) is twice as long as a half note (♩);

a half note (♩) is twice as long as a quarter note (♩);

a quarter note (♩) is twice as long as an eighth note (♪).

All rests are assigned time values, but we DO NOT play a rest, we just count its value:

A whole rest (▬) is twice as long as a half rest (▬);

a half rest (▬) is twice as long as a quarter rest (𝄽);

a quarter rest (𝄽) is twice as long as an eighth rest (𝄾).

o	whole note	= 4 beats	= ▬	whole rest
♩	half note	= 2 beats	= ▬	half rest
♩	quarter note	= 1 beat	= 𝄽	quarter rest
♪	eighth note	= 1/2 beat	= 𝄾	eighth rest
♬	sixteenth note	= 1/4 beat	= 𝄿	sixteenth rest
♬	thirty-second note	= 1/8 beat	= 𝅀	thirty-second rest
♬	sixty-fourth note	= 1/16 beat	= 𝅁	sixty-fourth rest

*These examples are all based on a quarter note getting one beat.

CLEFS:

Drum music is usually written in the bass clef: 𝄢

It may also be written in the neutral clef: 𝄥 which indicates that the lines and spaces designate

no specific pitch. Some percussion instruments are written in the treble clef: 𝄞

HOLDING THE STICKS:

Two different methods of holding the drum sticks may be used when playing from this book:

"MATCH GRIP"

Right Hand: with your palm facing down, pick up the drumstick between your thumb and first joint of finger number 1. The stick should rest diagonally across the palm of your hand with the first joint of finger number 1 and your thumb acting as a fulcrum. Now, gently curl the last three fingers around the stick, but NOT too tightly.

Left Hand: Repeat the same procedure as for your right hand.

"TRADITIONAL GRIP"

Left Hand: Starting with your hand palm facing up, lay the drumstick diagonally across your palm with the stick resting between your thumb and finger number 1, and also between finger number 2 and finger number 3. Gently curl fingers number 1 and 2 until they are lightly resting on the stick.

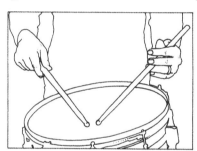

Right Hand: Follow the same procedure as the right hand of the "Match Grip."

Exercises

Continue this exercise for several minutes.

Continue this exercise for several minutes.

Suggestions

Alternate your strokes in all exercises in part one of this publication, so that if you start with the left hand the next note will be played with your right hand.

A practice pad is reommended for the exercises in this book, except when you advance to the rock patterns, which should be played on a drum set.

Counting out loud will help develop accuracy and coordination between our counting and playing.

Be sure to keep the flow of beats very steady. A steady rhythmic flow is most important.

TIME SIGNATURES:

Time signatures tell us a great deal about how a piece of music is to be played. They indicate how to count each individual measure. Measures are separated from each other by bar lines, so we will find a bar line at the beginning and end of each measure. A double bar line indicates the end of a section or total piece of music. A time signature is found at the beginning of a piece or section of music. The top number tells us the number of beats in each measure; the bottom number tells us the kind of note that will recieve one beat.

Example 1:

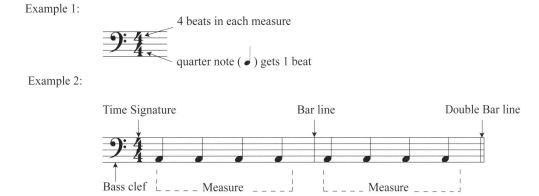

Example 2:

Many different time signatures can be used in music:

$$\frac{5}{4} \quad \frac{6}{8} \quad \frac{7}{4} \quad \frac{9}{8} \quad \frac{3}{8} \quad \frac{6}{4} \quad \frac{7}{8}$$

ACCENTS:

Accents (>) are used often in music and indicate when a note is to be plaed stronger (louder) than others.

In the above example the accents are located above beat number 2 and beat number 4, so these notes should be played louder than beats number 1 and number 3.

DOT:

A dot receives half the value of the note in front of it. A dot DOES NOT receive a drum stroke, you merely count its value.

Example:

In the above example you strike the drum on beat number 1 and beat number 4. Since the half note receives two counts and the dot receives one count (half the value of the note) you hold the dotted half note for three beats, then again play on beat number 4.

REPEAT SIGNS:

Two types of repeat signs will be used in this book. The one type tells us that when we play to 𝄇 we go back to 𝄆 and play it again. The other type of repeat sign 𝄎 tells us to play the previous measure again.

PART I-A
Quarter Notes

Since these exercises are written in 4/4, the top number tells us that there are 4 beats in each measure and the bottom number tells us that a quarter note (♩) receives 1 beat. The same is true for the quarter rest (𝄽), but rremember we DO NOT strike the drum on a rest—merely count its value.

Two 12 Measure Exercises

Alternate Hands

Notice in the next exercise that the foot will play different patterns than the hand.
This is to build foot and hand coordination.

PART I-B
Eighth Notes

Since 2 eighth notes equal 1 quarter note (♪♪ = ♩), an eighth note receives half of a beat, and is counted as follows:

The same is true for the eighth rest (♪), but remember that we DO NOT strike the drum on a rest.

Eighth notes are played twice as fast as quarter notes.

DYNAMICS:

Not all music is played at the same degree of loudness. These degrees of loudness (volume of sound) are called *dynamics*. Dynamics are indicated on the music in the following ways:

p = soft   *mp* = moderately soft   *mf* = moderately loud   *f* = loud   *ff* = very loud

Two 12 Measure Exercises

Advanced Eighth Note Exercise

Eighth Note Combined with Eighth Rest Exercises

NEUTRAL CLEF:

As was mention earlier, drum music is sometimes written in a neutral clef:

-- snare drum on 3rd space.
-- bass drum on 1st space.

The neutral clef merely indicates that the lines and spaces have no specific pitch. So, from this point on in the book you will find both bass and neutral clefs being used.

Two 12 Measure Exercises

Advanced Eighth Note Exercise

PART I-C
Sixteenth Notes

Since a group of four sixteenth notes equals one quarter note (), a sixteenth note receives one-fourth of a beat, and together they are counted as follows:

The same is true for the sixteenth rest ( ), but remember that we DO NOT strike the drum on a rest. Make sure that each sixteenth note or rest is of equal length (duration).

ANOTHER VERSION OF REPEATED MEASURES:

We have learned and understand that the symbol (𝄎) indicates a repeat of the previous measure.

The following symbol (𝄎) indicates that the *two* previous measures should be repeated.

Therefore:
(written)　　　　　　　　　　　　　　　　　　　(played)

9.

10.

11.

12.

13.

14.

15.

16.

17.

DYNAMIC CHANGE:

A gradual increase in dynamics (loudness) may be designated on the music by merely writing *"Crescendo"* (*cresc.*) under the part at a particular place.

A dynamic increase may also be indicated as: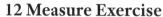

Concentrate on playing notes first, then play the notes plus dynamics.

12 Measure Exercise

"**C**" stands for Common Time. It is actually the same as 𝄴.

FIRST AND SECOND ENDINGS:

Repeats, as you have already learned, may be indicated in various ways. There is, however, another version known as the "first and second ending" which may be used:

Play from the ‖: to the repeat sign in the first ending. Then return to the ‖: . This time skip the first ending and go directly into the second ending.

Advanced Exercise

Notice the sixteenth rests (♪) in this exercise. Remember, we DO NOT play on a rest—merely count its value.

PART I-D
Dotted Eighth and Sixteenth Notes

We have already learned that a dot receives half the value of the note in front of it, and a sixteenth note receives one-fourth of a beat. Therefore, a dotted eighth note followed by a sixteenth note equals a quarter note (♪. ♪ = ♩) and is counted as follows:

Notice that you play on "1" and on "a" only.

DYNAMIC CHANGE:

A gradual decrease in dynamics (loudness) may be designated on the music by merely writing *"Derescendo"* (de*cresc.*) under the part at a particular place.

A dynamic decrease may also be indicated by an indication such as:

Concentrate on playing notes first. Then play the notes plus dynamics.

Two 12 Measure Exercises

Study With Repeat

Advanced Exercise

PART I-E
Triplets

An eighth note triplet consists of 3 *equal* eighth notes to be played *evenly* in the same time (one beat) as 2 eighth notes ( ), and is counted as follows:

12 Measure Exercise

A Short Etude (study)

Advanced Exercise

PART I-F
Eighth and Sixteenth Note Combinations

In this section we use the notation: ♪♫. Since an eighth note receives one-half of a beat and each sixteenth note receives one-fourth of a beat, this figure is counted as follows:

Notice that we DO NOT play on ⓔ. We DO play on "1," "&," "a" only.

Also used in this section is the figure ♫♪, which is counted as follows:

Notice that we DO NOT play on ⓐ. We DO play on "1," "e," "&" only.

16 Measure Exercise

D. C. AL CODA ⊕:

"D. C." (Da Capo) means go back to the beginning of the piece of music. "al Coda ⊕" means to play until you come to "To Coda ⊕," then junp directly (without delay) to the "Coda" (which means tail, tag, or ending.

16 Measure Etude plus Coda (⊕)

Advanced Exercise

PART I-G
Review Exercises

The next exercises use all of the notes learned in Part I. By combining these various notes we form many different rhythmic patterns.

Second Review Exercise

Third Review Exercise

Fourth Review Exercise

PART II-A
Hand Exercises

The following exercises are designed to develop hand dexterity.

Sforzando or *sforzato* are directives commonly applied to a note, indicating that it is to be performed with special stress, or marked for sudden emphasis. Such indications may be indicated in either of the following ways:

PART II-B
Three Stroke Ruff

This rudiment is one of many principles of learning drums and hand control. Notice that there are three sticking variations. Be sure to practice each version with equal devotion. If practiced correctly Part II will help you develop fine hand control and coordination.

Remember, maintain a very steady tempo and observe all accents faithfully.

[Give the definition of rhythm some serious thought. Discuss it with other people involved in music. Merely one definition is: "The organization of musical notation in respect to time."]

[There are accents made at any dynamic level. We perform notes marked to be stressed in soft sections as well as in louder passages, but not usually with the same amount of force.]

[Shading of dynamics is referred to as "performing nuances." The subtle (not too obvious) use of dynamics to make a phrase (musical sentence) more interesting is known as nuance.]

[You should experience the differences in sound and playing feel by using different weight sticks on the snare drum. Various sounds can be achieved by the use of different style sticks.]

A drum will sound different when played at various areas of the head. The center of the head vibrates for the shortest period of time. As the stick hits the head closer to the rim, the head rings more. Generally a drum is played near the center which usually produces a crisp sound at this area. However, you should experiment and probably work to get various tonal shadings. Also use these on a set of drums as fills across your Tom-Toms.

PART II-C
Four Stroke Ruff

In Part I of this book we learned that an eighth note triplet ( ) consists of 3 evenly played eighth notes in the time of a quarter note. ( ).

A sixteenth note triplet ( ) consists of 3 evenly played sixteenth notes in the time of an eighth note ( ).

TIME SIGNATURE 𝄴 ------- Six beats in each measure

------- Eighth note gets one beat

There are two ways to count ⁶₈ time.

(1) Six beats are in each measure if an eighth note is thought of as receiving one beat:

(2) Two beats are in each measure if a dotted quarter note is thought of as receiving one beat (or three eighth notes getting one beat):

[Compound Time is defined as any meter signature in which each beat in the measure is divisible into three—as we count ⁶₈ in two.]

PART II-D
Five Stroke Ruff

R L R L R   L R L R L

To play the five stroke ruff we merely add one more note to the four stroke ruff.

In $\frac{6}{8}$ time, since an eighth note receives one beat, a sixteenth note receives one-half beat and is counted as follows:

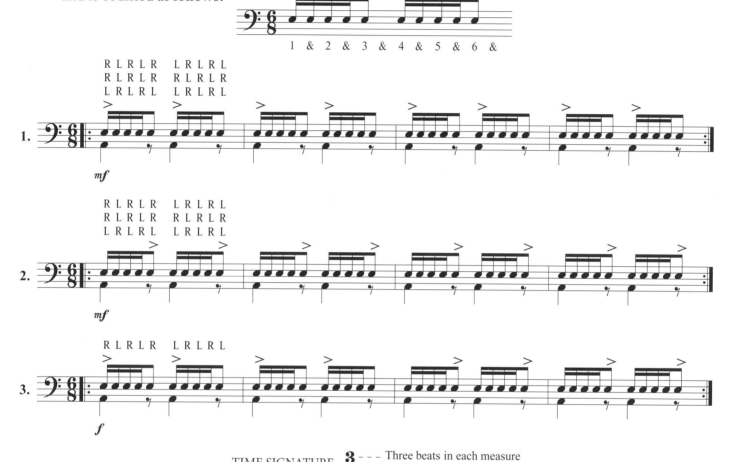

TIME SIGNATURE $\frac{3}{8}$ - - - Three beats in each measure
- - - Eighth note gets one beat

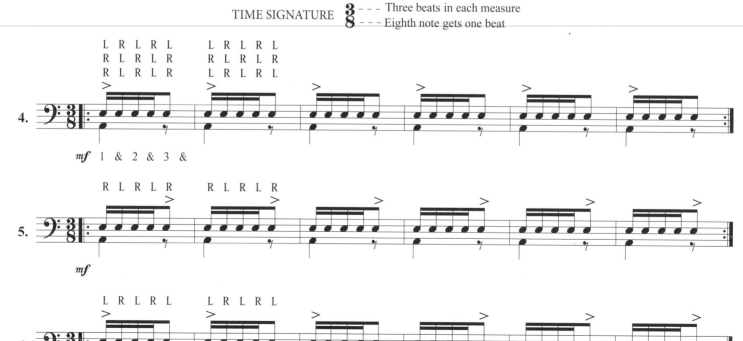

PART II-E
Five Stroke Roll

A double stroke roll (rudiment) is executed by playing two consecutive strokes with each hand. Even and steady counting is always a factor to be considered most important.

The five stroke roll is counted as the five stroke ruff is, except that we use double strokes (two consecutive notes with the same stick).

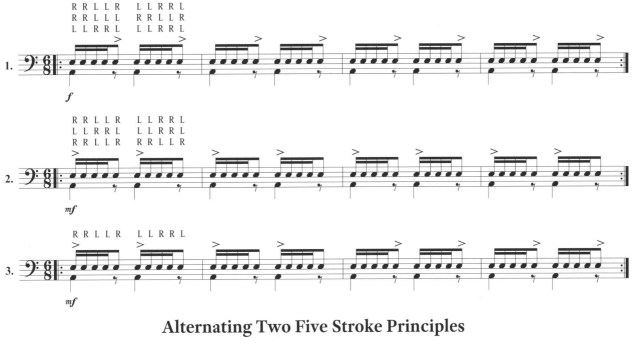

Alternating Two Five Stroke Principles

[Listen to the sounds you are playing. The faster you lift the sticks from the head, the more the head will vibrate and the better your drum sound will be.]

PART II-F
Seven Stroke Ruff

To play the seven stroke ruff we merely add two more notes to the five stroke ruff.

In $\frac{6}{8}$ time, since an eigth note receives one beat, a sixteenth note receives one-half beat and is counted as follows:

[If an exercise or piece of music appears with no drum stickings indicated you may choose your own. In the majority of cases you will most likely alternate strokes. However, getting a certain sound and rhythmic feel should determine your choice of sticking.]

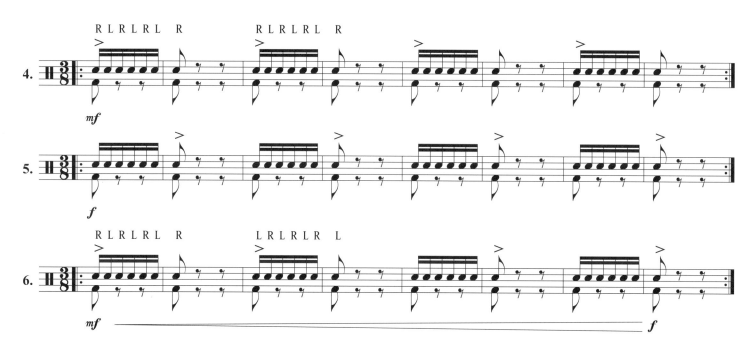

PART II-G
Seven Stroke Roll

Consider the fact that playing two notes with the same stick produces a somewhat different sound than alternating strokes. But, remember to keep all strokes even in volume and speed.

The seven stroke roll is counted as the seven stroke ruff is, except that we use double strokes (two consecutive notes with the same stick).

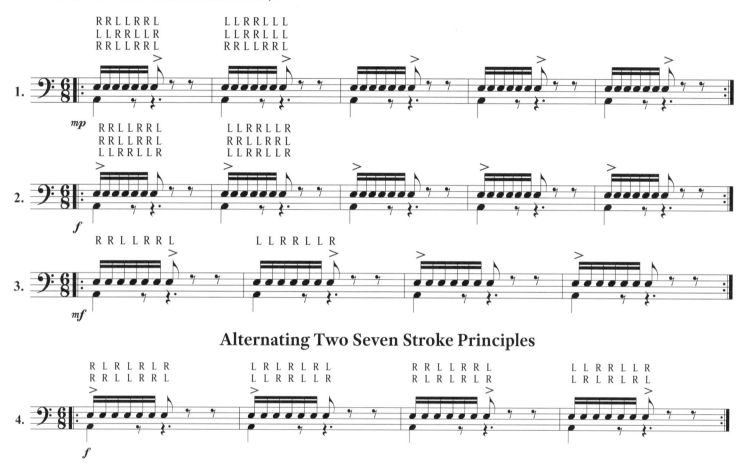

Alternating Two Seven Stroke Principles

[Remember: The bead (tip of the stick) must leave the head of the drum as soon as possible. The head must be allowed to vibrate with the shortest possible stick contact.]

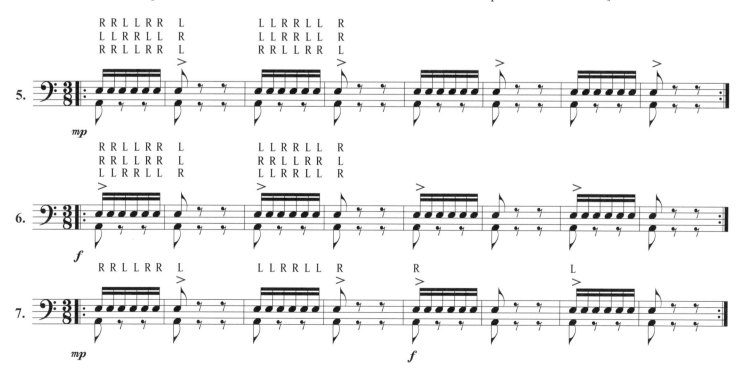

PART II-H
Double Stroke Accents

The following exercises should be used to develop hand and wrist control as well as muscular dexterity. The stress patterns, correctly learned, will enable you to play accents in all styles and in various groupings. Repeat each exercise many, many times to insure complete command.

[Snare drums and bass drums are never thought of as being tuned to a definite pitch, but are tuned for quality of sound (tone) and response by increasing or decreasing the tension on the head. While these instruments are occasionally used separately, they are usually played as a team.]

PART II-I
Mixed Sticking

These exercises are designed to develop the art of using mixed sticking. Control of wrists and hand muscles is a most important phase of becoming a fine drummer. You should practice each exercise repeatedly. Start with fairly slow tempi. A faster rate of speed may be set as your facility improves.

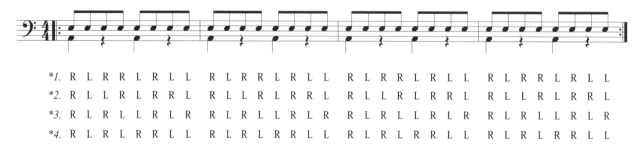

*1. R L R R L R L L   R L R R L R L L   R L R R L R L L   R L R R L R L L
*2. R L L R L R R L   R L L R L R R L   R L L R L R R L   R L L R L R R L
*3. R L R L L R L R   R L R L L R L R   R L R L L R L R   R L R L L R L R
*4. R L R L R R L L   R L R L R R L L   R L R L R R L L   R L R L R R L L

*Exercises with an asterisk in front of them are good Rock beat rhythms. To expand your performance abilities on these exercises you might try playing a cymbal with your right stick, using your left on the snare drum. Right foot plays the same pattern as your right stick.

5. L R L R L L R R L R L R L L R R L R L R L L R R L R L R L L R R

6. R L R L R R L R R L R L R R L R R L R L R R L R R L R L R R L R

7. R R L R L L R L R R L R L L R L R R L R L L R L R R L R L L R L

8. R L R L R L L R L R L R L R L R L R L R L R R L L R L R L R L R L R R L

9. R L R L R R R L L R L R L L L R R L R L R R R L L R L R L L L R

10. R L R L R L L L R L R L R L L L R L R L R L L L R L R L R L L L

11. L R L R L R R R L R L R L R R R L R L R L R R R L R L R L R R R

12. R L R L R R R R L R L R L L L L R L R L R R R R L R L R L L L L

13. R R R R L L L L R R R R L L L L R R R R L L L L R R R R L L L L

14. R L L L R L L L R L L L R L L L R L L L R L L L R L L L R L L L

15. R R R L R L L L R R R L R L L L R R R L R L L L R R R L R L L L

Mixed sticking studies are so very important for the developing drummer. Make each stroke with a well controlled bounce and be sure to get the stick away from the head as soon as possible. Repeat each study literally dozens of times.

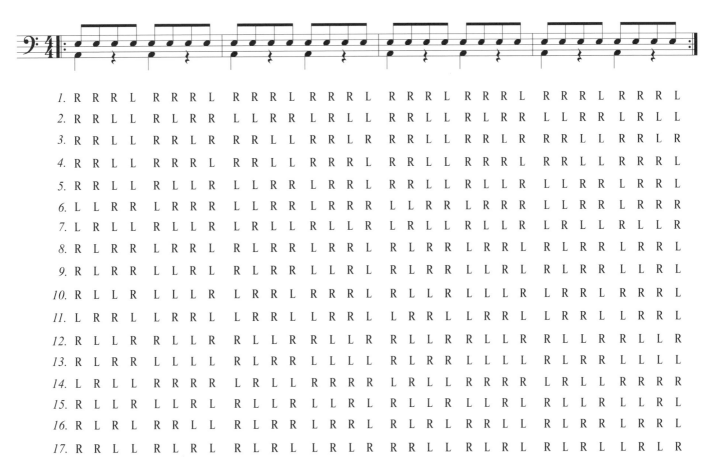

1. R R R L R R R L R R R L R R R L R R R L R R R L R R R L R R R L

2. R R L L R L R R L L R R L R L L R R L L R L R R L L R R L R L L

3. R R L L R R L R R R L L R R L R R R L L R R L R R R L L R R L R

4. R R L L R R R L R R L L R R R L R R L L R R R L R R L L R R R L

5. R R L L R L L R L L R R L R R L R L L R R R L L R R L R L L R R R L

6. L L R R L R R R L L R R L R R R L L R R L R R R L L R R L R R R

7. L R L L R L L R L R L L R L L R L R L L R L L R L R L L R L L R

8. R L R R L R R L R L R R L R R L R L R R L R R L R L R R L R R L

9. R L R R L L R L R L R R L L R L R L R R L L R L R L R R L L R L

10. R L L R L L L R L R R L R R R L R L L R L L L R L R R L R R R L

11. L R R L L R R L L R R L L R R L L R R L L R R L L R R L L R R L

12. R L L R R L L R R L L R R L L R R L L R R L L R R L L R R L L R

13. R L R R L L L L R L R R L L L L R L R R L L L L R L R R L L L L

14. L R L L R R R R L R L L R R R R L R L L R R R R L R L L R R R R

15. R L L L R L R L R L L L R L R L R L L L R L R L R L L L R L R L

16. R L R L R R L L R L R R L R R L R L R R L R R L R L R R L R R L

17. R R L L R L R L R L R L L R L R R R L L R L R L R L R L L R L R

[Every snare drum is equipped with a set of snares which should rest firmly against the bottom head when the tension lever is in "on" position. When the snares are released (lever in "off" position), the resulting sound is similar to that of an American Indian Tom-Tom or folk-type drum.]

PART II-J
Accented Triplets

The following exercises, very rhythmic triplets, should be strongly accented where indicated, or rim shots might even be used. Also, if practicing these studies on a drum set equipped with tom-tom, you might wish to play all accented notes on the tom-tom to further develop your facility.

[If a tom-tom is used, as suggested on the previous page, you should consider—
although not an instrument of definite pitch—that this instrument be tuned
lower than your snare drum, but not as low as your bass drum.]

A snare drum, often called side drum, has either a wood or metal shell. At each end of the shell is a parchment or plastic head. The top head is called the batter head—that on which the player performs; the bottom head is usually much thinner and is obviously called the snare head.

PART II-K
D.S. 𝄋 al Fine

Dal Segno: Return to sign and play to *Fine*
(*dal* = from; *segno* = sign)

Two Triplet Etudes

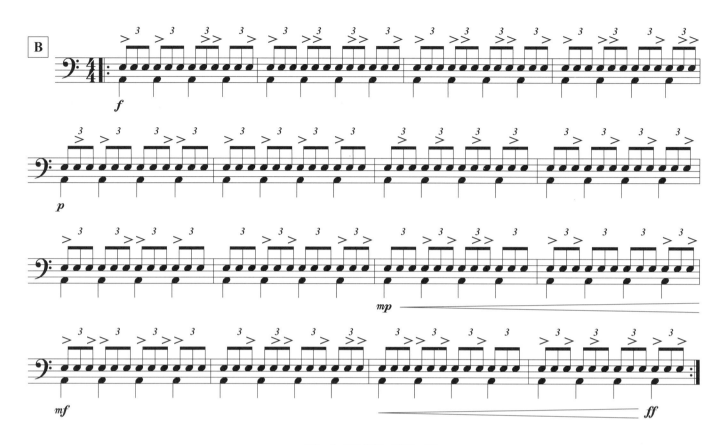

PART II-L
Advanced Triplet Exercises

PART III-A
Rock Pattern Exercises

This, the third part of the book, consists of all the various types of notes, rests, dynamics, etc. which were introduced previously. These many items are integrated into the following studies as modern Rock patterns.

A few simple abbreviations are used in these next pages which are:

S.D.   (Snare Drum)
B.D.   (Bass Drum)
Cym.   *(Cymbal)
H.H.   (High-Hat)

*[In this book, cymbal refers to a cymbal suspended from a stand.]

(cymbal quarter note)   (cymbal eighth notes)

You may wish to practice counting these rock rhythms before using the instruments to perform them. In the following example the numbers (vocal or hand counts) are on the beat and the "×" of each count is a foot tap (pedal beat).

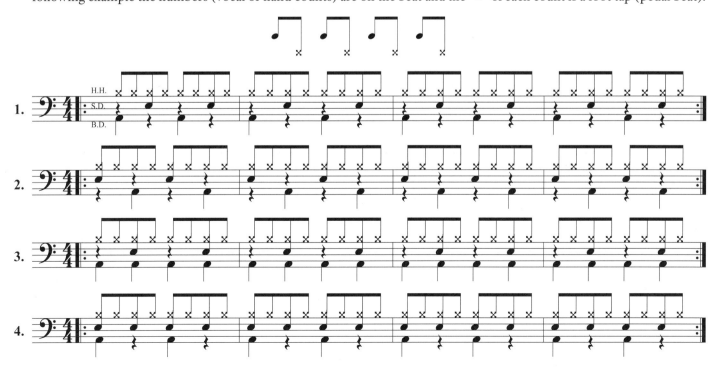

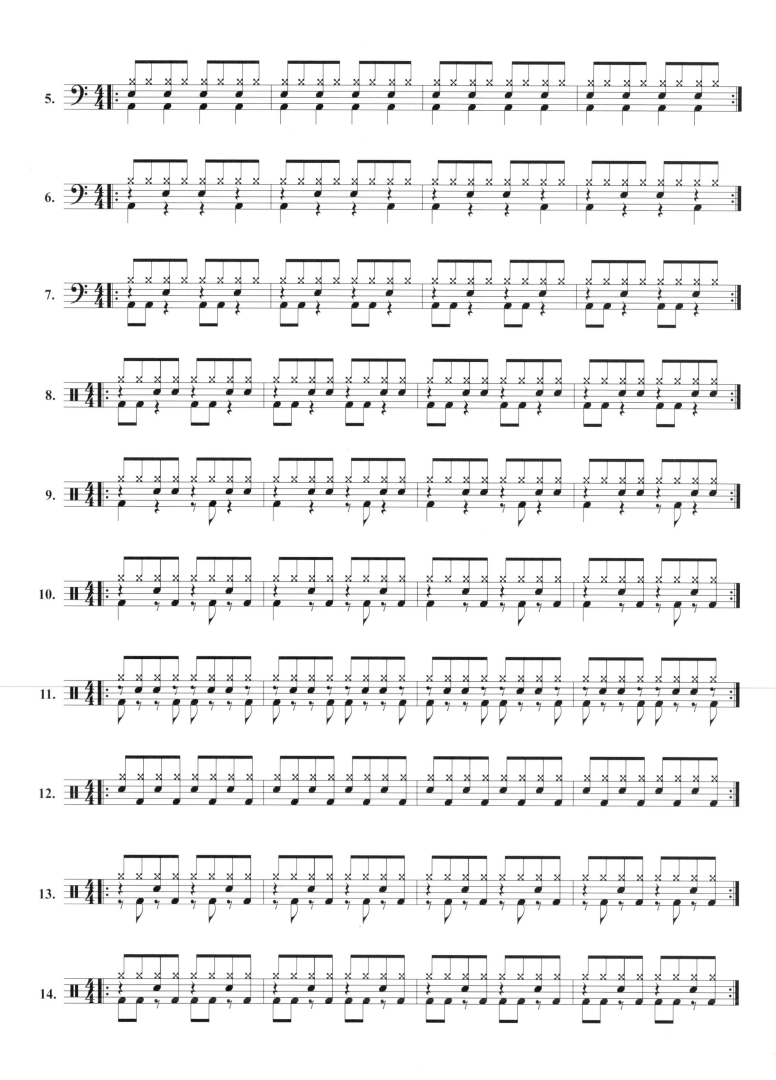

Rock Etude No. 1

PART III-B
Rock Pattern Exercises

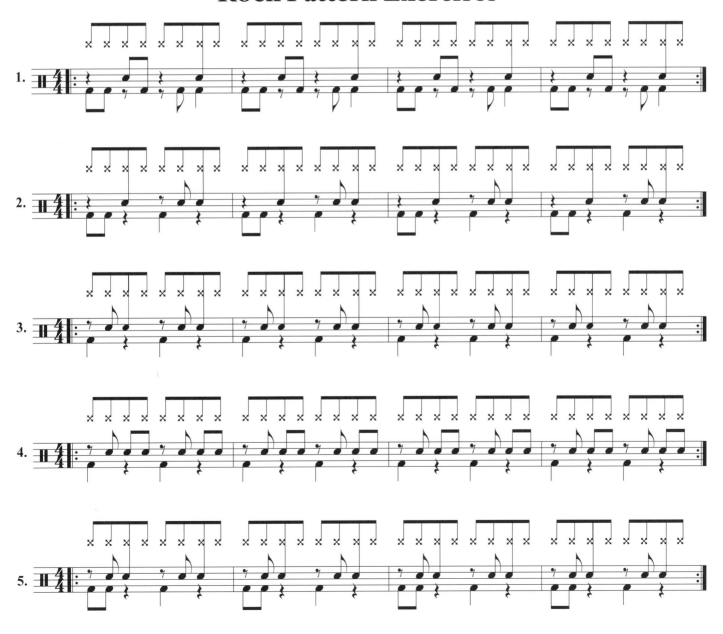

Rock Etude No. 2

PART III-C
Shuffle Exercises

Shuffle